Aboriginal Canadian Communities
HURON-WENDAT COMMUNITY

TRUE NORTH

BY TODD KORTEMEIER

True North is published by Beech Street Books
27 Stewart Rd. Collingwood, ON Canada L9Y 4M7

www.beechstreetbooks.ca

Produced by Red Line Editorial

Photographs ©: Robert Wagenhoffer/Corbis, cover, 1; Les Palenik/Shutterstock Images, 4–5; Pierre-Olivier Fortin CC2.0, 7, 8–9; Tom Hanson/The Canadian Press/AP Images, 11; Mathieu Nivelles CC2.0, 12–13; Val Lawless/Shutterstock Images, 14; Tony Moran/Shutterstock Images, 16–17; Hemis/Alamy, 18; Pierre-Olivier Fortin CC2.0, 20; Rainer Lesniewski/Shutterstock Images, 21

Editor: Amanda Lanser
Designer: Laura Polzin
Content Consultant: Dr. Kathryn Labelle, Assistant Professor of Aboriginal History, University of Saskatchewan

Library and Archives Canada Cataloguing in Publication

Kortemeier, Todd, 1986-, author
     Huron-Wendat community / by Todd Kortemeier.

(Aboriginal Canadian communities)
Includes bibliographical references and index.
Issued in print and electronic formats.
ISBN 978-1-77308-001-7 (hardback).--ISBN 978-1-77308-029-1 (paperback).--
ISBN 978-1-77308-057-4 (pdf).--ISBN 978-1-77308-085-7 (html)

     1. Huron Indians--Juvenile literature. 2. Huron Indians--Social life and customs--Juvenile literature. 3. Huron Indians--History--Juvenile literature.
I. Title.

E99.H9K67 2016   j971.004'97555   C2016-903118-7
                                                 C2016-903119-5

Printed in the United States of America
Mankato, MN
August 2016

TABLE OF CONTENTS

Chapter One

HISTORIC AND CURRENT LANDS

The word *Wendat* means "peninsula people." Wendat people in other parts of North America spell it Wyandot or Wyandotte. French colonists called the Wendat First Nation *Huron*. The word means "wild boar" in French. The colonists believed the hair of the Wendat people looked like the hair of a boar.

The Wendat have lived in many places. Before Europeans arrived in North America, Wendat lived in the St. Lawrence Valley. Their territory stretched between Lake Huron and Lake Ontario. It was a huge area.

Ancestors of modern Wendat people lived off the land. They fished, hunted, and gathered wild plants.

Many Wendat communities settled along the shores of Lake Huron.

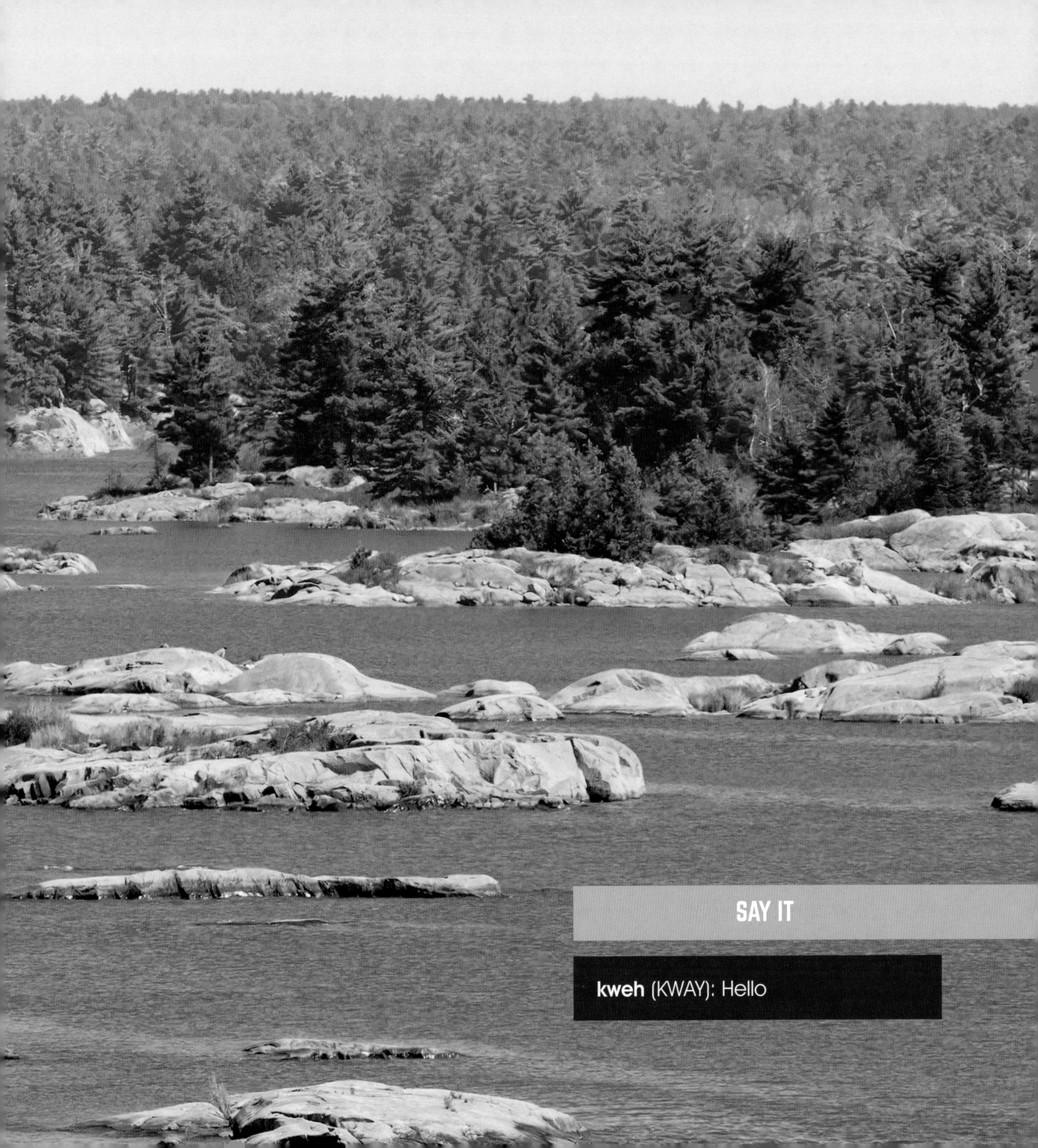

SAY IT

kweh (KWAY): Hello

They grew crops such as corn, beans, and sunflowers. Wendat women made baskets and pottery. They used and sold what they made.

EUROPEAN ARRIVAL

Wendat history is marked by conflict. They defended themselves against the Iroquois **Confederacy**. This was a group of several First Nations communities. When Europeans arrived, the Wendat **allied** with the French. The Iroquois Confederacy allied with the British. Conflict broke out, as did illness. Europeans had introduced new sicknesses to North America. Approximately 60 percent of the Wendat people died between 1615 and 1650.

In reaction, the Wendat moved to new lands across North America. Around 1650, some Wendat moved near Quebec City. Later other Wendat moved to land in modern-day Ontario and Michigan.

MODERN HURON LAND

Two communities of Wendat exist today. The first is the Wyandot of Anderdon Nation. Its people live along the border between Ontario and Michigan. The Wendake **reserve** is the second community. It is near Quebec City. Three thousand people live there. Wendake blends the proud history of the Wendat with modern society. Its museum

A typical street in the Wendake reserve

celebrates **traditional** Wendat life. Wendake residents hold traditional **ceremonies** every year. People come from all over to watch.

Modern Wendat hold the same jobs as other Canadians. Many continue to make and sell their traditional crafts.

Chapter Two

DAILY AND FAMILY LIFE

Traditionally, Wendat families lived in **longhouses**. A typical longhouse was 8 metres wide. But a longhouse could be any length. The longest one ever found extended 94 metres. Multiple families lived in each longhouse. Inside, there were sleeping platforms but few walls. The houses had several fireplaces.

Approximately 900 to 1,600 people lived in a typical Wendat village. A group of **elders** helped make community decisions. The Wendat were farmers. The quality of their land mattered a lot. They moved every few decades when the land started producing fewer crops.

A modern re-creation of a traditional Wendat longhouse

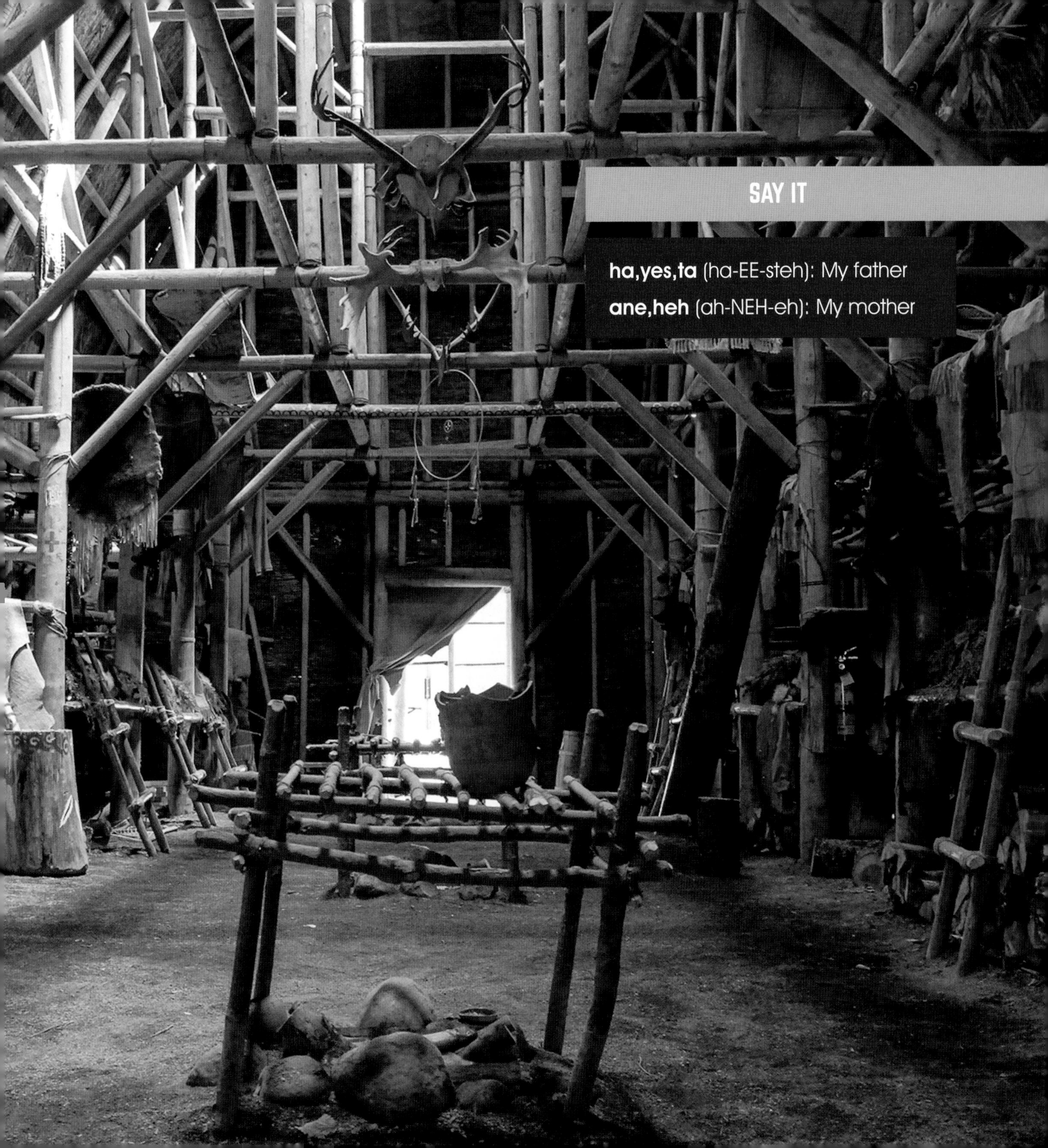

SAY IT

ha,yes,ta (ha-EE-steh): My father

ane,heh (ah-NEH-eh): My mother

Corn was a major part of the Wendat diet. They used corn to make flour and bread. They also made corn soup. Women and men both planted crops. Men also hunted and fished.

Modern Wendat no longer build longhouses. They live in modern apartment buildings and houses. But the longhouse is still very important. Examples exist today for people to go see. Sainte-Marie among the Hurons is a historic site near Midland, Ontario. It dates back to the 1600s. It shows what Wendat life was like.

CHILDREN AND EDUCATION

The whole village helped raise children. Wendat children received structured training. They learned about Wendat spiritual beliefs. They practised skills to become better hunters, farmers, and community members.

But in 1876, Canada passed the Indian Act. It created residential schools for First Nations children. The schools did not allow students to speak their native languages. Students could not practise their **cultures**. Some schools were open until 1996. Many Wendat traditions were lost. Few Wendat today speak the Wendat language. Most speak English and French. But some Wendat communities have

In 2008 Canadian Prime Minister Stephen Harper, standing, officially apologized for Canada's residential schools for Aboriginal Peoples.

language programs. The programs teach younger Wendat people the Wendat language.

Today, many Wendat children attend public school. Most Wendat children in Quebec attend the Wendake reserve school. They learn Wendat culture and traditions as well as math, reading, and science.

Chapter Three

SPIRITUALITY AND CELEBRATIONS

The Wendat are a very spiritual people. They believe everything has a spirit. This includes both living and non-living things. One traditional ceremony is the marrying of a pair of fishing nets. Tradition says if the nets are happy, they will catch more fish together.

Wendat spiritual leaders are called shamans. Shamans can be men or women. A village's shaman can have a few different roles. He or she might try to heal the sick. Some claim to control the weather. Others predict the future. The Wendat believe shamans have a lot of power. They are highly respected members of their communities.

Many Wendat communities use sweat lodges in certain rituals.

The Green Corn Festival celebrates the corn harvest.

The French introduced the Wendat to Catholicism in the 1600s. Today many Wendat practise this religion. Others in Southern Ontario are Methodist. But traditional ceremonies and healers are important to many modern Wendat people. They continue to celebrate their traditional spirituality and ceremonies.

FEASTS

Feasts are very important to the Wendat. They hold feasts for many different reasons. The Green Corn Festival is a special time. Each fall, Wendat give thanks for the corn harvest. They hold a feast to thank

14

the Creator for corn. They hold curing feasts for people suffering from illnesses. Dying feasts help Wendat say goodbye to loved ones when death is near.

The Wendat also celebrate the Feast of the Dead. It is held every 10 to 15 years. The Wendat dig up those who have died since the last ceremony. They rebury them together with others from allied First Nations. The Wendat believe this allows the souls of the dead to move on together into the afterlife.

POWWOWS

A powwow is an important celebration for many First Nations. In the past, Wendat held powwows to celebrate war victories. Today, powwows celebrate traditional Wendat culture.

The Wendake reserve holds a powwow every summer. Wendat demonstrate dances. They compete for who can dance the best. They wear traditional dress, including feathers and painted faces. Dancers perform to traditional music. Drumming is an important part of Wendat music. Drums create the beat for traditional dances.

Chapter Four

TOOLS AND TECHNOLOGY

The Wendat people are known for their expert canoe making. Wendat canoe makers use the bark of birch trees. Their canoes are up to 7 metres long. They are 1 metre wide. They can carry up to five people and 90 kilograms of goods.

The Wendat canoe is shaped for river travel. Its flat bottom is ideal for shallow water. It is very sturdy and stable. Construction methods have been passed down for generations. Until the 1970s, several canoe makers sold their boats in Wendake. These canoe makers are no longer in business. But many Wendat still enjoy canoeing and canoe making for recreation.

Wendat canoes are large and able to carry heavy loads.

INQUIRY QUESTIONS

Where did the Huron-Wendat people live in the 1600s? Where do they live now, and why did they move?

A Wendat woman wearing traditional clothing at the Huron-Wendat Museum in Wendake

FISHING AND HUNTING

The ancestors of modern Wendat people put their canoes to frequent use. The Wendat were skilled at fishing. They used nets and underwater traps called weirs. Small fish were caught in hand-held nets. For larger fish, Wendat set nets overnight. In the morning, they gathered up the catch.

Fishing was more important to the Wendat than hunting. But they did hunt deer and small animals. They made their own weapons. The Wendat used bows and arrows to hunt deer. They also hunted squirrels and rabbits. They made their own **spears** and knives. In the winter, Wendat hunters used snowshoes and **toboggans** to get around.

CLOTHING

Most traditional Wendat clothing is made from animals. Women **tanned** hides. They made clothes out of deer and beaver skins. In winter, they wore fur. Fur-covered leggings and sleeves kept the Wendat warm. **Cloaks** added further warmth. Women wore animal-bone combs in their hair. They also decorated with beads and body paint. Red was a common colour among the Wendat. Men carried items in pouches on their backs. One of these items was a pipe for **tobacco**. Pipe smoking was an important activity for the Wendat.

Today Wendat do not wear their traditional dress often. But it is a significant part of their history. During powwows and other celebrations, this sort of dress is still worn. Pipe-smoking is still part of important discussions and ceremonies. Life for Wendat today is different from the past. But the community continues to celebrate its heritage.

WENDAT TERRITORY

Wendat territory traditionally lay between Lake Ontario, Lake Erie, and Lake Huron. It expanded north into southern modern-day Quebec and Ontario.

Today, Wendat have one reserve, the Wendake reserve. It is in Quebec City.

The Wendake reserve is in Quebec City.

20

HUDSON BAY

QUEBEC CITY ◉

TORONTO ○

N
W ✦ E
S

◼ HISTORICAL
HURON-WENDAT TERRITORY

● HURON-WENDAT
TERRITORY TODAY

◉ CITY

ATLANTIC
OCEAN

GULF OF MEXICO

21

GLOSSARY

ALLIED
united

ANCESTORS
relatives of a person who lived a long time ago

CEREMONIES
formal events or acts with special meaning

CLOAKS
items of clothing that wrap around the body for warmth

CONFEDERACY
association of nations

CULTURES
beliefs, art, and customs of different groups

ELDERS
people whom the community respects as leaders in teaching cultural values

LONGHOUSES
homes where several families lived in one building

RESERVE
an area of land set aside for First Nations

SPEARS
weapons with long handles with sharp points at the ends

TANNED
made animal hide into leather

TOBACCO
a plant with large leaves that are dried and smoked

TOBOGGANS
long, light sleds

TRADITIONAL
according to beliefs passed on from one generation to another

TO LEARN MORE

BOOKS

Banting, Erinn. *Cree*. Calgary: Weigl, 2008.

Goldsworthy, Kaite. *Saskatchewan*. Calgary: Weigl, 2014.

Gurtler, Janet. *Teepees*. Calgary: Weigl, 2013.

WEBSITES

PLAINS CREE
LIBRARY AND ARCHIVES CANADA
https://www.collectionscanada.gc.ca/settlement/kids/021013-2161-e.html

SICC ANIMATION PROJECT FOR YOUTH
SASKATCHEWAN INDIAN CULTURAL CENTRE
http://www.sicc.sk.ca/sicc-animation-project-for-youth.html

TERMINOLOGY AND USAGE
UNIVERSITY OF OTTAWA
http://www.med.uottawa.ca/sim/data/Aboriginal_Intro_e.htm

23

ABOUT THE AUTHOR

Todd Kortemeier is a journalist, editor, and children's book author. He has authored dozens of books for young people on a wide variety of topics.